GOLF LEGENDS

CHELSEA HOUSE PUBLISHERS

GOLF LEGENDS

ARNOLD PALMER

William Durbin

CHELSEA HOUSE PUBLISHERS
Philadelphia

Produced by Daniel Bial and Associates
New York, New York

Picture research by Alan Gottlieb
Cover illustration by Bill Vann
Frontispiece photo: Arnold Palmer

First Printing

1 3 5 7 9 8 6 4 2

Library of Congress Cataloging-in-Publication Data

Durbin, William, 1951–
    Arnold Palmer / by William Durbin
        p.   cm.   — (Golf legends)
    Includes bibliographical references and index.
    Summary: A biography of one of the best-known golfers in the
    country, whose loyal fans are called "Arnie's Army."
        ISBN 0-7910-4562-5 (hc)
    1. Palmer, Arnold, 1929–   —Juvenile literature. 2. Golfers—United
    States—Biography—Juvenile literature. [1. Palmer, Arnold, 1929–
    2. Golfers] I. Title. II. Series.
    GV964.P3D87   1998
    796.352'092—dc21
    [B]   97-43915
                                                              CIP
                                                               AC

CONTENTS

GOING FOR BROKE

"**W**hat other people consider careless and foolish is my normal game," Arnold Palmer once said. "It is my nature to hit the ball hard and to go for everything. My whole philosophy has been based on winning golf tournaments, not on finishing a careful fifth or seventh or tenth."

Going for broke—risking it all on one big drive or a boldly struck putt—is the heart of Arnold Palmer the golfer as well as Arnold Palmer the man. He lives with passion, and puts his heart into every single thing he does. Whether he's making a charge in the final round of a golf tournament or raising money to help critically ill children at his Arnold Palmer Hospital in Orlando, Florida, Arnie gives it his all.

Of all the championships in Palmer's storied career, the 1960 U.S. Open at Cherry Hills in Denver, Colorado, stands out as the classic exam-

Arnold Palmer throws his sun visor in the air after wining the 1960 U.S. Open.

ple of his will to win. Going into the final round, Arnie was in 15th place. To make his situation more impossible, the names ahead of him on the leader board included some of the greatest players in history: Ben Hogan, Sam Snead, Julius Boros, Mike Souchak, and a 21-year-old newcomer named Jack Nicklaus.

Since Arnie was trailing leader Mike Souchak by seven shots with only eighteen holes to go, everyone counted him out of the tournament. Everyone, that is, except Arnold. "I had a hunch I could still win," he said, "if I started strong and got the ball rolling."

Arnold knew the first hole, a short but tough par four, was the key to scoring well, and he shared his feelings with sportswriter Bob Drum over lunch: "If I drive the green and make an eagle or a birdie," Arnie said, "I could shoot 65 this afternoon. What would that do?"

"Nothing," Drum laughed at Palmer, "You're too far behind."

"It would give me 280," Arnie insisted. "Doesn't 280 always win the Open?"

"Yeah," a second writer, Dan Jenkins, joked, "when Hogan shoots it."

Arnie left his hamburger on his plate uneaten and stalked away. Tight-lipped and angry at not being taken seriously, he walked straight to the practice range and hammered a few balls as hard as he could. Then Arnie strode to the first tee with his driver in hand. Putting aside the fact that he'd tried to drive this green and failed in each of the first three rounds, Arnie had made up his mind to go for it all one last time.

Though the 346-yard, par-four first hole at Cherry Hills was downhill, the landing area was so tight that even the longest hitting pros were afraid to take a chance on driving the green. To make the shot even tougher, a thick patch of rough blocked the front of the putting surface.

With his whole tournament hinging on one swing, Arnie lashed at the ball. The crack of Arnie's club head echoed like a pistol shot in Denver's mile-high air. His fans—known affectionately as Arnie's Army—turned their heads to watch his trademark draw fly straight and true. When Arnie's ball ran through the rough and on to the green, a cheer went up from the gallery.

As Arnie hitched up his pants and walked down the fairway, his fans followed close behind. Two putts later Arnie had his birdie, and a second huge roar echoed out over the hillside. Arnie and his Army were officially on the march.

The charge continued when Arnie canned a 35-foot chip in on the second hole. Then on the par-four third hole, he boomed a big drive that landed just short of the green. A perfect pitch and a one-foot putt gave him his third straight birdie.

Arnie made it four in a row on the next hole, when he hit a wedge to fifteen feet and hammered a putt into the heart of the cup. After a "mere" par on the fifth hole, Arnie deuced the 174-yard, par-three sixth hole by knocking in a tricky 25-foot putt.

By the time he got to the seventh hole, Arnie's gallery was even larger than normal. People who'd heard about his charge had run from every corner of the course. Responding to the occasion, Arnie made a six-foot birdie putt. He was now six under par after only seven holes.

Pars on eight and nine gave Arnie a 30 on the front nine and a chance to win the tournament.

Palmer has been one of the most popular golfers ever. Here he is greeted by fans in his hometown of Latrobe, Pennsylvania, after winning his second Masters in 1960.

Not one to let his Army down, Arnie scored two under on the back, parring the tough finishing holes that would later be the downfall of both Hogan and Nicklaus. Arnie's final round total of 65 made the former paint salesman from Latrobe, Pennsylvania, the United States Open Champion.

Arnie's charge at Cherry Hills, which was described by golf historian Herbert Warren Wind as "the most explosive stretch of sub-par golf any golfer has ever produced," was only the beginning for the young pro. Arnie's Army was now on the march, and the summer of 1960 marked the beginning of a run that would last for half a decade and ultimately crown Palmer king of the fairways and make him golf's first million-dollar man.

2
DEACON'S BOY

Though Arnold Palmer could make an extra $100,000 a year by wearing a cap with a company logo, he prefers a simple Latrobe Country Club visor. Why? Because it reminds him of his roots, and where Arnie came from is very much a part of who he is.

Arnold Daniel Palmer was born in Latrobe, Pennsylvania, on September 10th, 1929, only a month before the stock market crashed. Growing up as a child of the Depression, Arnie learned to value simple virtues such as honesty and hard work. His mother, Doris, was a lively lady who encouraged him to be friendly and outgoing, while Arnold's father, Deacon, was a stern man who taught Arnie respect and humility.

"My father didn't just teach me to play golf, he taught me discipline," Arnie recalls. "It wasn't the kind of discipline that says what you can't

Arnold Palmer grew up on a golf course, because his father was the superintendent and head pro of a course in Latrobe, Pennsylvania.

do—don't do this, or don't do that. It was the kind that said what you had to do—always do everything as hard and as well as you can."

Deacon was both course superintendent and head professional—the hard times dictated rolling two jobs into one—at the Latrobe Country Club, and his family lived in a small home that bordered the golf course. Deke, as he was fondly known by the community, gave Arnold his first set of cut-down golf clubs when the boy was only four years old. Although Arnold hit balls around his yard and often took casual lessons from his father on the practice range, as a nonmember of the club, he wasn't allowed on the golf course during regular hours.

"Hey, Pap, watch this," little Arnie would yell to his father from the range as he smacked the ball with all his might. "Pap! Watch! Pap!"

Although Arnie's energy wore on his father's patience at times ("You'd get so sick of him," Deacon later admitted), he quietly encouraged young Arnie to hit the ball with all his strength. Purists at the club urged Deke to train his son to swing smoother and with better balance, but he ignored them. "He'll balance himself better when he gets older," Deacon said, "and he'll hit the ball hard."

As the son of a working-class man—a golf course professional in those days was not a high status occupation—Arnold could play golf only early in the morning or late in the evening, after the members had concluded their rounds. Arnold fondly remembers the times he did sneak out on the course as a little boy: "I remember walking down the third hole, with my toy six-guns strapped on my hips and a golf bag over my shoulder, hoping Dad wouldn't catch me and give me hell for being out on the course during the day."

Growing up as a nonmember of Latrobe, Arnie always felt a little like an outsider: "I grew up in a country club atmosphere but was never able to touch it. It was like looking at a piece of cake and knowing how good it was, but not being able to take a bite. It was sort of a frustrating thing for me." Even the country club swimming pool was off limits to Arnie. "I could beat them all in golf, but I couldn't swim in the club pool, for instance. I had to go down to the stream."

On the days when Arnie wasn't allowed to play golf, he spent much of his time watching the members tee off on Latrobe's difficult sixth hole, which was directly across the road from his home. Arnie took to sitting on the side of the tee, studying the members' swings. One day a lady asked little Arnie if he could help her out by hitting her ball across a ditch that crossed the fairway about 125 yards out.

Tempted by the offer of a nickel—big money in those days—he smacked her ball over the troublesome hazard. Anxious for more nickels, young Arnie was quick to come to the aid of this and any other lady who might need a "pinch hitter." He admits he may have even become a pest: "That was an invitation I probably wore out, because I was on that tee every time that lady came by. And if anyone else needed help getting across that ditch, I was there."

From the age of eleven on, Arnie worked as a caddie at the club, happy to earn the standard 15-cent fee for nine holes. To this day he remembers his astonishment when a member generously paid him 35 cents for a single round. When

*Palmer (back right) has his
hand around the shoulder of
his friend Bud Worsham after
they played in a junior tournament in 1947.*

he wasn't caddieing, Arnie shagged balls for Deacon. He also learned all about golf course main-
tenance, spending long hours cutting the grass,
raking bunkers, and digging ditches.

As greenskeeper, Deacon worked right alongside his crews, showing the men by example
what he expected from them. Since Arnie spent
so many hours at his father's side, one of his
earliest memories is of Deacon and his tractor.
As a kid of only three or four, he would sit
between his father's knees on the big tractor seat
and ride all over the course.

It wasn't long before Arnie was mowing the

fairways on his own: "Some people think I developed my strong arms by working in the steel mills around Latrobe. Not so. I got them by working on the tractor for Pap. As I went chugging up and down those hills, it took everything I had—standing straight up and heaving the wheel with both arms—to horse that machine around."

By playing golf with the other caddies and spending his free time hitting balls out of the rough, Arnie quickly developed into an exceptional golfer. His practice in the rough—the only part of the course he was allowed to play on during the day—taught Arnie to hit recovery shots of every kind imaginable. He hit off one foot. He hit from pine needles, leaves, branches, and tangled grass. And as he played, he imagined himself in a tension-charged moment. "I'd be out there among the trees and I'd say, like a sports announcer, 'Here's Arnold Palmer in the trees at the right of the eighteenth hole at Augusta. He needs a birdie to win the Masters. . . . He swings— and there it goes! Right up to the cup and in.'"

From the start, Deacon trained Arnie to stay with the power golf swing he'd used from the time he was a little boy. "Always hit the ball hard," he'd say, and before Arnie reached junior high, he could outdrive nearly every man at the club. As much as he loved to drive the ball, Arnie also spent countless hours on his short game, chipping and pitching and putting long into the evening. Even the cold Pennsylvania winters didn't slow him down. "I'd go out and shovel off the back lawn in the winter," he said, "and hit balls that Pap painted red."

With his power and deft touch, Arnie was soon beating every caddie at the club. Arnold was also talented at both football and baseball, but once he entered high school, he shifted his focus to golf. Bill Yates, Palmer's high school coach, is modest in recalling his star pupil's career: "I didn't teach him anything. He knew more about golf as a freshman than anyone in school. He taught the team. I managed it."

What impressed Yates most about Arnold was his dedication to practice. "If he hit a bad five-iron shot in practice," Yates recalled, "he'd get a bag of 50 balls and bang away at the five-iron shot. Most kids went out to play. Arnie went out to win."

Arnie led Latrobe High School to three straight state championships. He won the individual title, too, in his senior year and made a place for himself in the National High School Record Book. When he was only seventeen he won the first of his five West Penn Amateur Championships.

Recognizing their son's talent, Deacon and Doris encouraged Arnie by driving him to local and regional events. More often than not Arnie came out on top.

Not that there weren't some rough spots on the way. Like every young player, Arnie also learned to deal with the frustrations of golf. One day at a tournament in a nearby city, Arnie got mad and threw a club. Though he won the event, neither his father or mother said a word for most of the drive home. Finally Deacon turned to his son and said, "If you ever throw a club again, you'll never play in another tournament. That will be the last time you play competitive golf." Arnold had won the tournament and was expecting to be praised. Instead, he got a lecture that he remembered the rest of his life.

Arnold decided to attend Wake Forest University, in Raleigh, North Carolina, where he became best friends with Buddy Worsham, the younger brother of U.S. Open champ Lew Worsham. On the very first day they arrived at college, Arnie and Buddy played a match, shooting 67 and 68 respectively, on a course neither one of them had ever seen. According to Wake Forest coach Johnny Johnson, the boys loved competing with each other. "One day Buddy set a course record of 63 over at Raleigh, and he couldn't wait to tell Arnie about it." Johnson recalled. "Palmer just told him to hold on for a while. Then he went over to Raleigh and shot a 62 to break Buddy's record."

The other thing that sticks in Johnson's mind is Arnie's physical strength. "He was as strong in the hands and shoulders as anyone I've ever seen. We used to do a little wrestling, and he was strong as a bull. He'd take on Buddy Worsham and myself at the same time, and he could handle us both."

Arnold soon played his way to the number one position on the Wake Forest team. For the next three years, he and Buddy ripped up their opponents. Though this was a era of great college golf—Gene Littler, Don January, Ken Venturi, Art Wall, Harvie Ward, and Mike Souchak were all contemporaries—Palmer was undefeated for two straight years. And to cap his college career, in 1949 and 1950 Arnie took medalist honors at the NCAA tourney.

At that point, Arnie's life was about as perfect as any young man could hope. However, during his senior year, tragedy struck. One autumn night in 1950, Buddy asked Arnold to drive with him to a homecoming dance at nearby Duke University, but Arnie declined. A few hours later, Buddy was killed in a car accident.

Stunned by the loss and feeling guilty that he'd let Buddy go alone that night, Arnold accompanied his best friend's body back to the Worsham home in Washington, D.C. Long after the funeral was over, Arnold continued to blame himself. "I felt it wouldn't have happened," he said, "if I was along."

Wake Forest was never the same for Arnold after that. "I didn't know what to do with myself," he said. "I stayed in school until I thought I'd go crazy—every time I turned around to tell him something, I'd realize he was gone."

Though Arnold was only a semester away from a business administration degree, he withdrew from school and began a three-year hitch in the Coast Guard. His first assignment, Cape May, New Jersey, gave him a taste of flying, which was something he'd always wanted to try. Later, while on assignment in Cleveland, Arnold's love for golf was rekindled. According to Arnie, a number of his Cleveland friends had "a maniac appetite for golf," and they ended up playing every free minute, even on winter days when "the pins were frozen solid in the cup."

Following his stint in the Coast Guard, Arnold worked briefly as a painting supply salesman. He didn't want to become a club pro like his father, and he was convinced that a business career would let him play in enough amateur tournaments to satisfy his need for golf. However, in the summer of 1954, Arnold won his second straight Ohio State Amateur. He decided to give the United States Amateur Championship a try.

Arnold played well early in the week, defeating amateur stars Frank Stranahan and Don Cherry. In a tough 36-hole match, he squeaked

Palmer shows off some of the trophies he won while serving in the Coast Guard.

by Ed Meister by winning the third sudden death hole. The final paired him with Bob Sweeney, a former British Amateur champ and Royal Air Force pilot. Sweeney started off strong, birdieing the second through fourth holes to go three up. Through the rest of the 36-hole final, Arnie fought his way back. After some brilliant play by both players, Arnold finally surged ahead and took the lead for good on the 32nd hole.

Sports Illustrated celebrated 25-year-old Arnold Palmer's victory as a "battle of classes," with a mill town boy beating a "graying millionaire playboy who is a celebrity on two continents."

Palmer cheers after winning the National Amateur Championship in 1954.

Arnold's Amateur championship, which he still counts as the most treasured of all his wins, gave him the confidence to give the PGA tour a try.

On his way to the pro tour, Arnie got sidetracked by a pretty young girl named Winifred Walzer. He met her on a Tuesday at an amateur golf tournament in Delaware, and on Thursday, he proposed. Although Winnie's father was the president of a national canned goods corporation, Arnie never stopped to consider the fact that Mr. Walzer might not be interested in having a poor salesman who spent too much of his time golfing as a son-in-law.

Knowing he needed some cash to buy a ring for Winnie, Arnie accepted a wager from his boss back in Cleveland. His boss said he'd pick a par 70 course—one Arnie had never played before— and for every stroke Arnie scored under 72, he promised to pay the would-be groom $200. To make it more interesting, for every shot Arnie went over 80, he'd have to pay the boss $100.

It sounded like a great proposition. The problem was that the boss picked Pine Valley in New Jersey, a course that was open for 25 years before anyone broke par. To make matters worse, Pine Valley was tightly bunkered, while Arnie's home course in Latrobe had very few sand traps.

When Arnie bogeyed the first hole, the boss smiled. The bet was already turning in his favor. Realizing he needed to drive the ball long and straight to avoid the bunkers, Arnie turned on his patented power and attacked Pine Valley. Hole by hole, Arnie gained poise and confidence. By hitting the ball as hard as he could, he took the bunkers out of play. Arnie finished with a blistering 68—good for $800 and a down payment on a ring worthy of his new love.

Shortly after Arnie married, he began searching for someone willing to back him financially for his first year on the tour. After turning down several offers that required him to share his winnings, he won an endorsement from Wilson Sporting Goods Company. They agreed to loan Arnie all his golf equipment and provide him with around $2,000 in exchange for a three-year endorsement of their products. This money, along with some loans from his family and friends, gave him his start.

To this day Arnie is proud of how quickly he

Arnold Palmer checks out one of his drivers as wife Winnie looks on.

paid back those loans. He said, "It took me a year—but only one year—to pay them all back." As a child of the Depression, he knew too well how debt can destroy a man, and he was anxious to start his new life free and clear.

According to tour regulations, as a rookie Arnie was unable to earn any prize money for six months, no matter how well he finished. So he and Winnie were forced to scrimp and save. To avoid the high cost of meals and lodging, they pulled a travel trailer from one tournament to the next, hoping their old car wouldn't break down.

In June, Arnie finally started to bank some cash on the PGA tour. His 25th place in the Fort Wayne Open paid him $145. A third in St. Paul yielded $1,300, followed soon after by his $2,400 first-place check at the Canadian Open.

He wasn't anywhere near the top of the money list when the year ended, but he was confident he had the game to make it on tour. Arnie could hardly wait for the new season to begin.

3

KING OF AUGUSTA

Arnie's magical season of 1960 began at the Augusta National Golf Club, the site of the Masters Tournament. The spirit of Arnie's newly formed "army" of fans and the electric quality of his play helped to make the major championship tournaments of that year the stuff of legends.

Arnie brought excitement to every event he entered. Whether he came home with the trophy or not, Arnold made an impact. "Even in losing he is the thrilling and appealing new figure that golf has been awaiting," wrote Alfred Wright in *Sports Illustrated*.

Most golfers tried to conceal their emotions, but Arnie wasn't afraid to let his feelings show. His strong, expressive face became famous for its dramatic contortions. When Arnie frowned at a lipped out putt or a bad bounce, his whole gallery agonized with him. And when Arnie pumped his fist after ripping a drive or sinking

Palmer watches one of his trademark long drives.

a long birdie, the crowd shared his elation. They followed Arnie from hole to hole, straining at the gallery ropes and willing, as he willed, every shot to fly true and every putt to fall.

Feature stories in major newspapers and magazines praised Palmer as the new American hero. His physical strength, his winning smile, and his colorful personality endeared him to both the press and the public. Writers compared him to baseball's legendary Babe Ruth, to boxer Jack Dempsey, and to tennis great Bill Tilden.

Arnie was so honest and refreshing in his approach to the game that even his fellow professionals rooted for him. As Al Wright observed: "Palmer enjoys the sympathy and affection of his fellow players. If they can't win, they hope he will, and none begrudges him his sudden prestige and success."

From the time Arnold Palmer was a little boy, he dreamed of winning the Masters. Back at Latrobe he often told the members, "Some day I'm going to be a big golfer like Bobby Jones." The ladies and gentlemen of the country club would smile and nod, humoring the small boy with the big dreams.

The wide-open fairways of Augusta suited Arnold's power game. Arnie's first win at the Masters had come in 1958. After tying Sam Snead at the close of the third round, Arnie fought off a valiant Ken Venturi to win his first green jacket.

Though Palmer's win was a surprise in 1958, he played so well again in the 1959 tourney, that reporters picked him to win the following year. *Los Angeles Times* columnist Jim Murray, one of the many who admired the young golfer's flair for attack, said, "He doesn't play a golf course, he tries to obliterate it."

April in Georgia, as always, was bright and green. Arnie's opening 67 fulfilled everyone's expectations. His fans were ready to crown him king. However, he faltered over the next two days, carding a 73 and a 72.

By the time Arnie's touch came back to him on the final day, two veterans, Dow Finsterwald and Ken Venturi, had pulled ahead. Even though Arnie posted a three under 33 on the front nine, Finsterwald and Venturi still held a one-shot lead.

By the time Arnie got to the 12th hole, he was running out of time. Just ahead, Venturi had gone one up on Finsterwald, and it looked like the tournament was Ken's to win. At the height of this tension-filled moment, Arnie glanced at the scoreboard beyond the green and had to smile. In the corner of the huge board that was reserved for official messages, someone had posted a proclamation in capital letters: "GO ARNIE."

Meanwhile, Venturi defied the will of Arnie's fans and parred in. He now looked like the sure winner. CBS even briefed Venturi for his television interview, and tournament officials fitted him for the winner's green jacket.

When Palmer failed to birdie 13 and 15, two easy par 5s, his fans figured it was all over. Their faces mirrored Palmer's own disappointment as he trudged to the 17th tee, knowing he was down to his last few swings. Arnie now faced two of the toughest holes on the course, and he needed at least one birdie to get into a playoff. Pars, which were normally great scores on 17 and 18, would leave him stuck in second place.

Even though Arnie hit a solid drive on 17, his approach came up short, leaving him with a 35-

foot putt on a slick green. Palmer studied the situation. He could either lag it up for a safe two putt and try to get his birdie on 18, or he could try to sink this and go for the win on the final hole. If he tried to sink it and missed, however, he would possibly be forced to three putt, which would put him out of contention. Arnie's Army nervously looked away as their hero twice approached his ball and backed off.

When Arnold stood over his putt for the third time, he'd made up his mind. He would go for broke. "Never up never in—that's the way I looked at it," Arnie recalled. "If it was going to be a bad putt, it was going to be a spectacularly bad putt. For I wasn't going to fall short of the hole."

Arnie rapped his putt hard. Halfway to the hole the gallery knew the ball would roll clear off the green if he missed. But his line was true. A huge roar echoed out over the treetops of Augusta, as Arnie punched his fist in the air and trotted to the cup to retrieve his ball. His charge was on!

Although Arnie could have played safe on 18 and gone for par, the thought never crossed his mind. Giving his driver a solid rip off the final tee, he split the fairway. Cheers rose up on all sides.

Left with a full six iron to the green, he considered his approach with care. He wanted no less than a birdie, and to guarantee a makable putt on the tricky 18th green, he would need to hit it tight.

"Start deliberate," Arnold thought back to his father's advice on how to handle pressure situations, "and come back slow on the back swing. Then give it everything you've got on the down

swing."

That's exactly what Arnie did. Purely struck, his ball sailed straight for the target, landing just right of the pin, and spinning back to within five feet. The roars that went up from the mammoth gallery were only equaled by the roars that greeted Arnie a few minutes later when he hammered

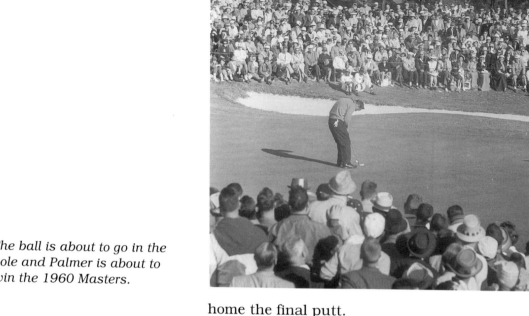

The ball is about to go in the hole and Palmer is about to win the 1960 Masters.

home the final putt.

One new development that made Arnie's charge at Augusta so special was the role of television. Expanded coverage allowed millions of fans across America to witness his victory. Arnie played the role of the hero so well that he became an instant celebrity—a symbol of strength and courage.

Television and Arnold Palmer arrived at the Masters, and together they created something that was more than the sum of their parts. The magic of that moment signaled the beginning of an era. No longer would athletes swinging golf clubs or baseball bats or tennis rackets be simply young men. Instead, following in Arnie's footsteps, they would become millionaires, marketed by the dream merchants of Wall Street and sought after by a world hungry for heros.

When Arnold Palmer was crowned king of Augusta late on that April afternoon, the fans who were lining the fairways joined company with millions more who were at home watching the drama unfold on television. Together they changed the face of professional athletics, and in the process they became the original members of Arnie's Army. To honor the occasion, *Life* magazine ran a headline that week, signaling the dawn of a new era in American golf: AT MAS-TERS, PALMER REPLACES HOGAN, SNEAD.

4

THE OPEN

Following his triumphs at Augusta and Cherry Hills, the next stop in Arnie's golden summer brought him to Scotland. Although there were other tournaments in between—Palmer won a total of eight titles worth a record $75,000 in 1960—it was clear from the beginning of the year that he had his sights set on the major championships. For after winning the Masters and the U.S. Open, Arnold knew that victories at the British Open and America's PGA tournament could bring him what no professional golfer had ever accomplished—a "grand slam" of all four majors in a single year.

Of all the national opens in the world, there is only one tournament that can be simply identified as the Open. The tradition of the British Open, which began in 1860, is unmatched in the golf world. Played at a rotating venue of the

Palmer went to Scotland in 1960 hoping to win the Grand Slam. Here he tees off during a qualifying round at St. Andrews.

finest courses in Scotland and England, this grand spectacle draws an international field to its annual contest for the Claret Jug.

However, by the late 1950s the reputation of the Open was at an all-time low. American professionals were making so much money that most of them saw no reason to travel all the way to Britain to play in one tournament. As a result, the quality of the field continued to decline, and so did the prestige of the tournament.

Then came the summer of 1960.

Deacon Palmer and his son had always talked about Arnold playing in the British Open. Out of respect for the game, Arnie believed that it was the duty of every man who made his living from golf to compete in the Open. "I had always planned to play in it once I felt I could afford to go abroad," Arnold said. "The fact is it's a championship that is just very important to any golfer who plays for more than what dollars and cents can get you. . . . You just really must play it if you're a true professional, and you love the game." And despite the continued poor attendance by other American pros, Arnold and his dad were soon winging their way across the Atlantic.

The site of the 1960 Open was the Old Course in St. Andrews, Scotland, the birthplace of golf. The British press had taken to Arnold Palmer's daring style, and they viewed him as a contender on the open, seaside links of St. Andrews.

Arnie's first task was to hire a caddie. Knowing he needed an experienced hand to give him a proper line for the many "blind" tee shots and to help him avoid the menacing pot bunkers of the Old Course, he enlisted a veteran bag carrier named Tip Anderson.

Arnie played his first practice round in gale force winds and shot an 87. His terrible front nine—a 48—was so discouraging that Arnold thought about walking in. But Tip talked him out of it, and he improved a bit more in every practice round after that.

Once the tournament started, Arnie continued to score a little better each day. Though he charged to a 68 in the final round, he lost by two strokes to Kel Nagle of Australia. Arnold was so gracious in defeat that the captain of the Royal and Ancient Golf Club praised him for adding "tremendous grace to a monumental battle." Arnold later admitted, "It was the biggest disappointment of my life." For no matter how well he played in next month's PGA Championship, there would be no chance for the grand slam this year.

As tough as the loss was to take, Arnold was encouraged by his play in the Open. He'd learned a lot about links style golf, and he was confident that he could improve his standing. "Arnold wanted to win badly the next year," his caddie, Tip, recalled, and he arrived at Royal Birkdale, the site of the 1961 Open, ready to do battle.

Arnie was at the peak of his game that summer, and he played steady right from the start. Though a gale blew up in the third round, Arnie shot a front nine 32, six shots better than anyone else. By the end of the day, it looked as if Palmer had a lock on the championship. However, while the rest of the players fell out of contention, Dai Rees, a stubborn Welshman, managed to stay close to Palmer. During the final round, Rees continued to play well, and by the last few holes, he'd pulled to within one shot of Arnie.

Palmer's wife and father flew over to Scotland to cheer Arnold on.

If Arnie ever needed a charge it was then. But disaster struck on the 15th hole. Arnie hit his tee shot too high, and a gust of North Sea wind pushed his ball into the heavy, tangled rough. To make matters worse, the grass was wet from two days of rain. Spectators who walked over to look at the lie could only shake their heads. Arnie had no choice but to pitch back into the fairway and give up a shot to Rees.

But Arnie had other ideas. "I took the six-iron and went for the green rather than play it safe," he recalls. "I tore into the shot as hard as I could, leaving a foot long scar in the rough."

The thousands of shots Arnie had practiced from the rough as a boy back at Latrobe paid off. The ball flew high and true. It was one of the greatest pressure shots in the history of championship golf—a plaque was later placed to commemorate his amazing recovery—and it left Arnie with an easy two-putt par. The momentum had now swung in Arnie's favor, and there was no stopping him. He finished birdie-par-birdie to win his first British Open by a single stroke.

His victory received rave reviews. British broadcaster Renton Laidlaw believed that Arnie's play singlehandedly restored the Open to its former glory. "It all happened because Arnold Palmer came," Laidlaw says. "He reestablished it as one of the four major championships, and the debt that Britain owes to Arnold Palmer is immense."

Palmer returned to Britain the next year and successfully defended his Open title at the Royal Troon course. That July, Arnie was at the top of his game, and he ran away with a six-shot victory. Even British fans, famous for their reserve, loudly applauded this dashing young "Yank's" display of talent and courage.

Palmer's lifelong Scottish caddie was equally forceful in praising Arnie. "He put the British Open back on the map," Tip said. "He's got character, charisma, and he's just a 100% gentleman. I've never heard anyone say anything bad about him. He's probably the greatest sportsman that ever lived."

5

THE REIGN CONTINUES

During the early 1960s, Arnold Palmer reigned unchallenged as the king of golf. Along with his back-to-back British Open victories, he won the U.S. Open once and finished second four times. Arnold also won the Byron Nelson Award, which is given annually to the player with the most tour victories, four years in a row. In addition, the Vardon Trophy, an award for the low scoring average on tour, went to Palmer four times in the 1960s.

At his peak, Arnie's patented final-round charges became the rule of the day. From 1960 to 1963, Palmer was in contention during the last round of 38 tournaments, and he won 29 of them—an incredible 76-percent success ratio. But of all the tournaments Arnie played in, the one he dominated most often was the Masters. In the seven-year period from 1958 to 1964, Arnie won the tournament four times, took sec-

Arnold Palmer taps his foot impatiently, waiting for his putt to drop at the 1962 Masters.

ond twice, and finished third once.

His even year wins at Augusta—1958, '60, '62, and '64—became as predictable as the coming of spring. Through the 1960s, America watched Arnie and the Masters grow up together. To help Arnie and "his" tournament along, television coverage expanded every year. The early broadcasts featured six studio cameras, brought outside just for the event and connected by bulky, one-inch cable laid across the ground. Today, 30 cameras, 300 workmen, 500,000 feet of underground cable, and a cluster of international satellite links all make the Masters Tournament one of the most watched sports productions in the world.

The Masters owes much of its popularity to Arnold Palmer. For it was Arnie's televised charges that mobilized armchair fans across the America and gave corporations a perfect audience for their ads. Business executives recognized that products identified with Arnold Palmer sold themselves, and they began offering huge endorsement contracts. Arnie's familiar face was suddenly worth millions.

During the same years that Arnie was winning with such flair, he also experienced some crushing losses. His defeats revealed even more about his character than his victories. Though Arnie hated to lose, he realized that his go-for-broke style could also lead to a catastrophe now and then. The thing that endears Arnold to his fans just as much as his championships, is the gentlemanly way he accepts his setbacks. And many of those setbacks were spectacular.

Arnie's classic "crash" occurred in the final round of the 1966 U.S. Open. He had a seemingly insurmountable seven-shot lead over Billy

Casper with only nine holes to play. Even Casper, his playing partner, admitted he would have been happy with a second-place finish.

Then Arnie got greedy. "I felt so confident of victory," Palmer said, "that I let my attention wander from the realities—winning this tournament—to pursuing another goal: beating the U.S. Open scoring record shot by Ben Hogan in 1948." Knowing that he'd set the British Open record a few years before, Arnie couldn't resist trying to do the same for our Open.

Arnie lost two shots to Casper early on the back nine, but he never considered the possibility that he might lose. It wasn't until Arnie went for a tricky pin on 15—still going for an Open record—and bogeyed, that he realized Casper could be a threat. Three poor tee shots later, Arnie had not only lost his chance for the record, but he'd also lost the Open.

After four rounds, three players were tied at the 1962 Masters. The playoff ended as Gary Player and Dow Finsterwald watched Arnold Palmer sink this putt to win.

Palmer lofts a ball from the trap at the Masters. Palmer won in Augusta, Georgia, every even year between 1958 and 1964.

Lesser athletes might have thrown down their clubs or stalked off the green without speaking to anyone. But Arnie remembered Deacon's lessons about respect and humility, and blamed no one but himself. "I cost myself the U.S. Open victory," he said. "I assumed I had the tournament won when that was not a fact."

This sort of conduct rallied more support than ever for Arnie. "People seemed to understand," Arnie said, recalling the loss. "The receptions I got in the weeks and months after that were warmer and bigger." His galleries swelled with new fans who wanted to see this brave battler. Whether he won or whether he fell victim to some cruel turn of fate, they wanted to be there to cheer him on.

Another tragicomic moment for Arnie came in the 1969 Los Angeles Open. Though he needed only a par for a 69 when he arrived on the par-five 18th hole, Arnie decided to go for the green in two. Why not? An eagle would give him a 67. After pushing one shot out of bounds to the right and hooking a second off the course to the left, Arnie still wouldn't put his three wood away. When he finally hit the green, he two putted for a fat 12. Being a good sport, Arnie later gave permission to the L.A. Junior Chamber of Commerce to put up a plaque on that spot, to give comfort to average golfers who often card 12s of their own on that hole.

Always willing to do anything he could for the little guy, Arnie proved he could take a joke as well as he could make a string of birdies under pressure.

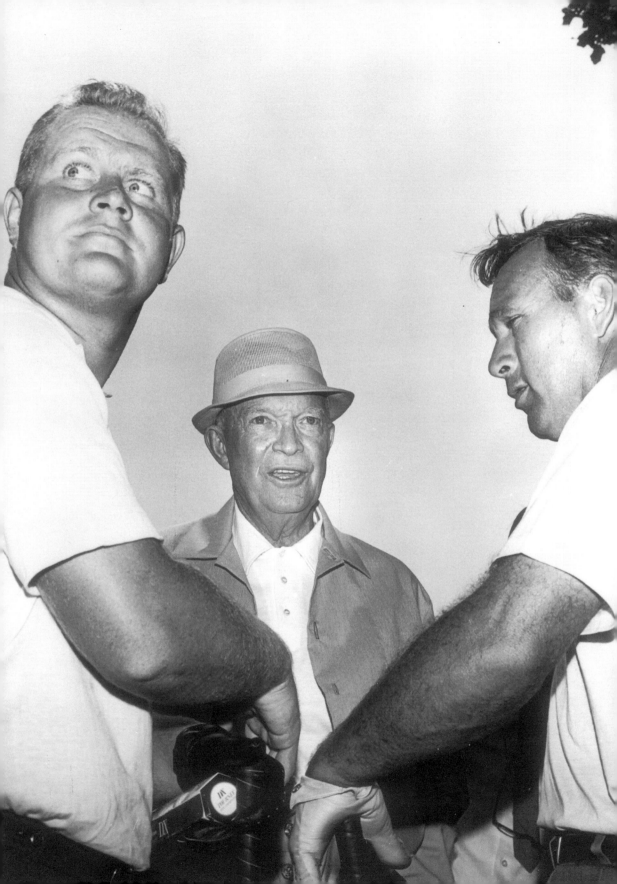

6

FLYING HIGH

In 1971, Arnold Palmer bought the Latrobe Country Club, bringing his life full circle. Arnie proudly returned to Latrobe as the owner of the golf course where he'd caddied in his youth. The kid who couldn't swim in the club pool now had the keys to the whole property. When Arnie was asked if he intended to keep Deacon on as head pro and greenskeeper, Arnie joked, "If he behaves himself."

Though Arnie purchased Latrobe for sentimental reasons, it also made good business sense with his multimillion dollar income. As his winnings, endorsement contracts, and investments grew through the 1960s, Arnie gradually found himself managing a small financial empire.

It all began when Mark McCormack, president of a management company called IMG, approached

One of the joys of golf is getting to know other people from different walks of life who also love the game. Here Jack Nicklaus (left) and Arnold Palmer (right) team up with war hero and former president Dwight D. Eisenhower, an avid golfer himself.

Arnie and offered to help organize his business affairs. Since paperwork was something that often distracted Arnie from playing as much golf as he wanted to, he was happy to have Mark's help. Their deal, sealed only with a handshake, has endured to this day, and both men have profited immensely.

McCormack especially enjoyed how easy it was to "sell" Arnie. "He had everything," Mark recalls. "He was attractive, and he lived the American dream. He was bold and daring, and he played golf like all of us would like to play if we had the courage."

Jack Nicklaus, Arnie's archrival, agrees with McCormack. "I think Arnie has been great for golf," Jack says, "with his energy, his charisma, his magnetism, his competitiveness, and his ability to capture a situation. Plus he came along at a perfect time. No one was dominating the game."

Millions of dollars were soon rolling in. But Arnie didn't let the money go to his head. "I never coveted prize money for its own sake," he says, "but because it would help me get to the next tournament and do what I most wanted to do: play golf better than anyone else in the world."

One thing that allowed Arnie to play more golf more places was flying. As soon as he earned enough money as a journeyman pro, he took flying lessons. From the time he was little, Arnie loved planes. "If there was anything that could compete with my interest in golf, it was flying," he said.

Arnie spent many hours as a kid building handmade model planes out of balsa wood, and he visited with pilots every chance he got. "When I wasn't building—and breaking—model planes,

I was running down the country club road to the airport. There was a flight room where some of the pilots would gather around an old potbellied stove, and I'd sit there listening to tales of the sky."

Palmer purchased his first plane, a twin-engined Aero Commander, in 1958, the year he won the Masters. He soon graduated to a Lear Jet, and today he flies a Cessna Citation VII jet aircraft, logging nearly 100,000 miles per year. He makes at least one annual trip to the Far East, where he is the most recognized of all celebrity endorsers. (Once when a 4:00 A.M. fire alarm emptied a South Pacific hotel, Arnie spent a half hour signing autographs and posing for pictures outside, even though he was only wrapped in a sheet.)

According to Arnie, the convenience of air travel allows him the freedom on a given day, "to fly from home to New York for a business breakfast and then to a exhibition in Georgia around lunch time and finally to our golf course in Orlando, Florida, for dinner." (Arnie owns a small course in Orlando, which, soon after he bought it, became the home of the Bay Hill Classic, an important annual event on the PGA tour.)

Palmer also likes flying because it offers a personal challenge. He is a skilled pilot who is licensed to fly multiengine aircraft, and he's flown "everything from a jet fighter to a 747." In 1976 he set a record for an around-the-world flight by a business pilot, circling the globe in only 58 hours.

Says fellow pilot Darrell Brown of Arnold: "He's a quick study in these matters. To qualify for an instrument rating, a pilot normally takes a 10-

day course under an FAA-rated instructor." But Arnie picked everything up "in about a day of intense study and instruction. And he was able to do it—under all the pressures of his life—because he brings to it the same concentration he brings to golf."

Along with his interest in flying, Arnie has also become a spokesman for an impressive array of Fortune 500 companies. Since 1960 he has represented no fewer than 200 corporations, including Cadillac, Rolex, Stouffers, and Pennzoil. The reason Arnie has been so sought after to do commercials is simple—people love and trust the man. Arnie insists on taking his endorsements seriously. He refuses to do advertisements unless he believes in the product and uses it himself. "I don't do endorsements as something where I say, 'Here I'm going to make some money.' I take them personally and always have."

Alastair Johnston, a Palmer aide, claims that the secret to Arnie's appeal is his amazing range. Young and old, male and female, rich and poor all admire Arnie. "He is appealing to the steelworker in Pittsburgh and to the very elite in Palm Springs," Johnston says, and "he has a well-earned reputation of honesty and credibility."

Palmer's own company, Arnold Palmer Enterprises, has over 300 full-time employees housed in three national offices. Under his famous ProGroup logo, Arnie markets sporting goods, golf-related products, and clothing on a worldwide scale. He has also pursued a lifetime interest in teaching golf through his Arnold Palmer Golf Academy.

Golf course architecture has become another of Arnold's interests. With the help of associate

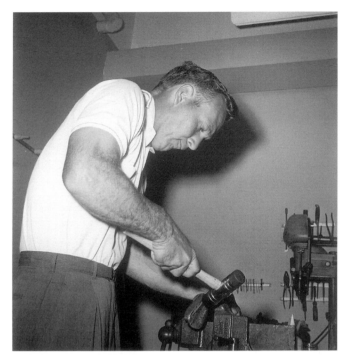

Palmer makes sure a club head is aligned just the way he likes it before heading off to a tournament.

Edwin Seay, his Palmer Course Design Company has built over 200 courses around the world. Arnie uses his lifetime of experience to guide his design teams and to supervise the on-site work.

Because of his overwhelming popularity and nationally recognized name, Palmer has often been approached with offers to run for political office. The governorship of Pennsylvania, a senate seat in Florida, and the presidency of the United States have all been mentioned to Arnie, but he always politely declines. "Not while I'm still active on the tour. Maybe in a few years I might consider it."

Though being a politician would certainly limit his golf—a thing Arnold could not abide—the reason most of his close friends give for Arnold's refusal to get to involved in politics is his integri-

One of Arnold Palmer's hobbies is flying, and he enjoys piloting his own plane from one tournament to the next. He started taking flying lessons in 1956 and in 1976 he (along with two other pilots) set a speed record for circumnavigating the globe.

ty—he's too honest. "He'd have trouble with the patronage and deal making," Arnie's good friend, Doc Griffin, bluntly says, "He's so damned honest, that would drive him crazy."

The stature of Arnold Palmer as a private citizen is best exemplified by his 1990 invitation to address a joint session of Congress, commemorating the 100th birthday of former president Dwight D. Eisenhower. Joining Arnie were Walter Cronkite; Ike's son, John; and Kansas senator Bob Dole—exalted company for a greenskeeper's son. Arnie delivered a brief speech in Ike's honor, the least he thought he could do, considering that the former president had once stopped by to surprise Arnie on his birthday, saying, "Any chance an old man can spend the night here?"

7

THE SENIOR TOUR

It is impossible to overestimate Arnold Palmer's contribution to the Senior Tour. Veteran golf writer Peter Dobereiner wrote: "Without Palmer, the senior tour would not have worked. The potent magic of Palmer was responsible for creating the most astonishing sporting success story of the 20th century."

Though Arnold has won only ten tournaments as a senior, his victory count is secondary to his charismatic personality. His appearance at a senior tournament, regardless of how he happens to be playing that week, guarantees the sponsors hundreds of thousands of dollars in ticket sales. It is primarily due to Arnold Palmer that the over-fifty circuit has become a multi-million dollar enterprise, changing from "a walk down memory lane" to "a walk to the bank."

The United States Golf Association, a group

In 1995, Arnie waved to his fans on the Swilken Bridge on the Old Course at St. Andrews. He had announced that he would no longer compete in the British Open.

which is infamously slow to change, even rewrote its age rules shortly before Arnold's 50th birthday to accommodate Arnie. By lowering the age requirement from 55 to 50 and making Arnie eligible to play, the USGA wisely took advantage of Palmer's worldwide marketing potential.

Despite the USGA's wishes, Arnie waited a year before he officially joined the Senior Tour. He simply didn't like the idea of getting old. At his 50th birthday party he seemed genuinely surprised that the time had finally come. "Fifty?" he said. "There's no way I can be that old." And for a year Arnie tried to prove that he wasn't 50, choosing to compete on the regular tour, even though his last victory, the 1973 Hope Classic, was already six years past.

When Arnie reluctantly agreed to give the senior side a try, his Army remobilized with a speed and enthusiasm that astonished the world of sport. The Senior Tour instantly became the place to be. Veteran pros who had been dreading the arrival of old age, were now counting the days to their 50th birthdays—the time they would, once again, be able to play alongside Arnie.

A glance at attendance figures for two U.S. Senior Opens shows what a phenomenal draw Arnie is. In 1979, the year before Arnie joined the senior tour, only 4,000 spectators attended the Senior Open Championship. However, with Arnold in the field the very next year, 43,000 cheering fans filled the galleries at Oakland Hills.

Old friend Lee Trevino speaks without a hint of resentment when he admits how popular Arnie is. "Arnold Palmer has more people watching him pack his trunk, than the rest of us do when we're leading a tournament," Lee says. "That tells you what an impact he's had on the game."

Though Arnold was a multimillionaire when the Senior Tour started and could have retired to a life of luxury, he wasn't about to let his fans down. "The galleries are important to me," Palmer said. "They're one of the reasons I'm still playing. Arnie's Army has changed a lot over the years, but it's still there. And I still have the drive to win."

In 1995, *Forbes* Magazine published a list of the wealthiest athletes in America. A 65-year-old Arnold Palmer finished fourth. His annual income of $13.6 million put him just behind basketball superstars Michael Jordan and Shaquille O'Neal. However, the portion of Arnold's multi-million dollar income that came from playing on the Senior Tour was a mere $35,000. In other words, he made $13,565,000 from other sources.

Despite the fact that it put very little money in his pocket, Arnold Palmer entered fifteen Senior Tour events in 1996 and five regular tournaments, including the AT&T, the Bob Hope Classic (he's a five-time winner), the Masters, the British Open, and his own Nestles Invitational at Bay Hill. Why play so much for so little? There are two simple reasons: his love of the game and his sense of duty to his fans. For not only does Arnold still love golf, but he also feels a responsibility to give something back to the fans who've supported him so loyally over the years.

Arnold recently became a major investor in the Golf Channel, and he is presently acting as chairman of its board of directors. Always anxious to do everything he can to promote golf, he's been taping promotional segments and special features about his life, his career, and his teaching theories. Since Arnie "invented" televised golf more than 30 years ago, he's the perfect man to lead the sport into the cable/satellite age.

Palmer still has enough new projects ahead of him to keep him busy for another 65 years. Work has always been his life, and that's the way he likes it. "Retirement is not a word in my vocabulary," Arnie has said on more than one occasion.

Though business enterprises are important to Arnie, golf remains the center of his life. And he still plays to win every time he tees up a ball. Appearing with regular tour players last year at Southern Hills, Arnie showed up on the range with his usual assortment of clubs—three sets of irons and five drivers—and began hitting balls. The younger players studied Arnie as he practiced, and Arnie often stopped to chat with them. A while later, superstar Nick Price looked at his watch and realized that Palmer had been practicing for four hours. "It dawned on me," Nick said, "that what made him special wasn't all the tournaments and awards he's won. It was his pure, unequaled love for the game. I hope and pray that when I'm his age I can enjoy the game as much."

Another thing that separates Arnie from the average golfer is his commitment to the future. He refuses to waste time agonizing over what might have been. He is proud of the way he has lived, and the way he has played golf. "I have never looked back at a golf tournament and said I would have changed the way I played," Arnie stated with pride. "That's my style. That's the way I got here, and that's the way I'm gonna go out."

A coffee table in the Palmer home symbolizes

Arnie's need to continually look forward. The walnut table is old and cracked, and it no longer fits the decor of the room, but Arnold would never dream of getting rid of it. For inlaid into the top of that table are Arnie's major championship medals: four from the Masters, two from the British Open, and one gold and four silvers from the U.S. Open. The telling feature of this table, however, is not the medals, but the one empty hole Arnold has left for his next victory. He always wanted it to be the PGA Championship, but even if he'd won that one, he would have immediately gotten out his drill. For every time Arnie won a major, he said, "we'd bore another hole into the table, and leave it empty for the next medal."

In January 1997, Palmer announced that he was undergoing surgery to treat cancer of the prostate. The surgery was a success, and doctors announced that they expected Palmer to recover fully and even be able to play again soon.

So even though Arnold Palmer has reached the twilight of his competitive career, there is still a place set aside in his heart for his next big win. And whenever or wherever that charge may happen, you can be sure that Arnie's Army will be waiting to cheer him on.

STATISTICS

TOURNAMENT VICTORIES

Year	Wins	Year	Wins	Year	Wins	Year	Wins
1955	1	1964	3	1973	1	1982	2
1956	4	1965	1	1974	0	1983	1
1957	4	1966	6	1975	2	1984	4
1958	3	1967	4	1976	0	1985	1
1959	3	1968	2	1977	0	1986	1
1960	9	1969	2	1978	0	1987	0
1961	6	1970	1	1979	0	1988	1
1962	9	1971	5	1980	2		
1963	9	1972	0	1981	1		

MAJOR VICTORIES - 7

REGULAR TOUR WINS - 60
SENIOR TOUR WINS - 10

CHRONOLOGY

1929   Born in Latrobe, Pennsylvania, on September 10.

1947   Becomes Pennsylvania state High School Champion.

1947   Enrolls at Wake Forest University.

1949   Wins first NCAA Championship.

1954   Wins United States Amateur Championship; joins PGA Tour.

1955   Wins the Canadian Open, his first pro victory.

1958   Notches his first Masters Championship; finishes the year as leading money winner on PGA tour.

1959   Wins first Byron Nelson Award for most tour wins (4).

1960   Wins United States Open Championship.

1961   Wins his first British Open Championship; wins his first Vardon Trophy for low scoring average on tour (69.95).

1962   Wins his third British Open and second Masters Championship.

1979   Joins Senior PGA Tour.

FURTHER READING

Aultman, Dick, and Ken Bowden. *The Masters of Golf.* New York: Macmillan Publishing, 1973.

Guest, Larry. *Arnie. Inside the Legend.* Orlando, Fla.: Tribune Publishing, 1993.

Palmer, Arnold. *Play Great Golf.* New York: Doubleday, 1987.

Palmer, Arnold, with Barry Furlong. *Go for Broke!* New York: Simon and Schuster, 1973.

Sampson, Curt. *The Eternal Summer.* Dallas: Taylor Publishing, 1992.

ABOUT THE AUTHOR

William Durbin is a graduate of the Bread Loaf School of English and has supervised writing research projects for the National Council of Teachers of English and Middlebury College. An avid writer and golfer, he teaches English at Cook High School in northeastern Minnesota and golf at Vermilion Fairways. His books include a young adult novel, *The Broken Blade*, and *Tiger Woods* in the Golf Legends series.

INDEX